SUMM
TRANS

The New Science of Self-Actualization

By

Scott Barry Kaufman

BlinkRead

Table of Content

DISCLAIMER:

This is a book summary of Transcend:
The New Science of Self-Actualization
By Scott Barry Kaufman and is not the original
book. This book is not meant to replace the
original book but to serve as a companion to it.

SYNOPSIS:

Transcend (2020) expands on Maslow's famous ideas about human needs and presents them in a new light that takes us on a path toward self-actualization. It explains the ways in which love, connection, creativity and purpose can be part of our lives. In addition to providing practical advice on how to become your best possible self, it also demystifies transcendence, explaining that it's something we can all integrate into our daily lives.

ABOUT THE AUTHOR:

Scott Barry Kaufman is a humanistic psychologist. He holds a PhD in cognitive psychology from Yale University and has taught at multiple prestigious institutions, including Columbia University, the University of Pennsylvania, and New York University. His previous books include Ungifted and Wired to Create.

INTRODUCTION.

Be the best self you can be.

If you've ever taken an introductory psychology class or followed a wellness blogger on Instagram, then you're probably familiar with Maslow's famous hierarchy of needs.

You've most likely seen a picture of a pyramid divided into five different levels. The bottom level, the base of the pyramid, represents humankind's most basic need: safety. The top level, the pyramid's tip, represents our most abstract need: self-actualization. This image makes it easy to think that going through life is like advancing through the levels of a video game: once you're done with safety you can forget about it and move on to the next level, until, eventually, you reach the last level – self-actualization.

This understanding is a bit simplistic. What's

more, Abraham Maslow himself was working on a deeper way to understand the whole of human existence when he died in 1970. These blinks expand on his work and reimagine it, showing how self-actualization is about integrating all your needs into a healthy whole that enables you to grow. They explain how realizing your full human potential can connect you not only to your best possible self but also to the people around you. Along the way, you'll learn that transcendence, far from being mystical, is something we can all aim for in our everyday lives.

You'll also find out

how getting lost in a good book gives you a taste of transcendence;
what a centenary on a remote Greek island can tell us about fundamental human needs; and
why seeking adventure is good for your mental health.

The need for safety is the basis of all other needs.

Ever been hangry? If you're like most people, you probably have, even if you're not familiar with the word. "Hanger" is hunger-induced anger, and though the word is obviously a humorous coinage, it points to a very real phenomenon.

It's just one example of how, when basic needs like hunger aren't met, negative emotions can overwhelm us, causing all other feelings and concerns to fade into the background.

Our most basic need is safety. Safety means stability, a sense of certainty, and having trust in our environment. It's the secure foundation that allows us to take risks and explore the world.

The key message here is: The need for safety is the basis of all other needs.

Beyond physiological needs like hunger, our sense of safety comes down to how we relate to the people around us.

One of the ways we relate to others is called attachment, and it begins in childhood. Every human is born helpless and completely dependent on the people taking care of it. An infant's sense of safety depends on its caregiver. If the caregiver is close and paying attention, the infant will feel safe and secure, and it will be willing to play and explore the world.

But if the caregiver leaves or stops paying attention, the infant will get anxious and start trying to get noticed again – by crying, for example.

From these interactions in infancy, we develop our attachment style. As we grow older, our attachment style plays a key role in our relationships. If we were lucky enough to grow up in a warm, caring environment, we learn to be attached in a secure way. We feel confident that others will accept us. But if our caregivers weren't reliable or sufficiently available, we become anxious in future relationships. We may even avoid close relationships altogether, which is called avoidant attachment.

No one's attachment style is completely secure. There's a broad spectrum between secure and avoidant, and most people have at least some levels of anxious or avoidant attachment – or both – especially in times of stress.

Still, people who have a secure attachment style are better equipped to deal with life's challenges. They cope with and regulate their emotions in more constructive ways, and have more satisfying relationships. In contrast, insecurity, especially the anxious kind, can lead to depression and loneliness.

The good news is that, though we learn our attachment style in childhood, we can change our patterns. New, positive experiences can help us develop healthier ways of interacting.

Connection is a fundamental need.

If you spend some time on the sunny Greek island of Ikaria and get to know its residents, you'll probably be invited to a hundredth birthday party or two. On this little island in the Aegean Sea, there's no shortage of centenarians. What's more, many of them enjoy active social lives.

The secret to their longevity? It's not just the nice weather and their healthy diet.

It's their close social ties. On Ikaria, people are convivial and caring. Neighbors care for each other, sharing food and celebrating together, and most people live with extended family instead of alone. In a word, there's a strong and reliable community.

The key message here is: Connection is a fundamental need.

Being around people – whether that means sharing a glass of wine or cooking a meal – fulfills a deep human need: connection with others.

The need for connection is the need for stable, positive, intimate relationships. In two words, it's the need for belonging and intimacy.

Let's look at belonging first. It comes down to being a part of a social group. The need for belonging is satisfied when you feel accepted by a particular group. When you feel rejected and invisible, in contrast, that need is unsatisfied.

Just how important the need for belonging is can be seen in what happens when it's not met. When you're excluded, it's not just your feelings that are hurt. Research shows that the pain of social rejection is indistinguishable from physical pain. And the effects don't end there. Continued rejection can lead to all kinds of problems, from poor sleep to depression.

But connection involves more than merely not being rejected. The quality of the connection also matters. That's where intimacy comes in. Belonging is about feeling protected by your group; intimacy is about loving, caring for and protecting others with whom you have a close relationship.

What makes for a quality connection?

Well, close connections hinge on what psychologist Carl Rogers calls unconditional positive regard. This occurs when each person feels seen, cared for, and safe expressing a whole range of feelings and experiences.

There is also mutuality in high-quality connections, which means that the people involved are engaged and participating. Such connections also encourage experiences that keep us coming back for more – laughter, joy, having fun together, and reciprocal gestures of kindness.

Healthy self-esteem is the result of positive accomplishments.

What image comes to mind when you hear the words "high self-esteem"? Do you instantly imagine a brash, arrogant narcissist who's constantly claiming the spotlight? In popular culture, self-esteem is often equated with an oversized ego. But healthy self-esteem is something else entirely.

Self-esteem is not the same as self-regard. It has nothing to do with narcissism or egocentricity. Rather, self-esteem is the natural result of genuine accomplishment and connection with other people. If you find yourself too focused on improving your self-esteem, that's already a sign that something has gone wrong.

The key message here is: Healthy self-esteem is the result of positive accomplishments.

Healthy self-esteem has two aspects: self-worth and mastery. Let's look at self-worth first.

In a nutshell, it comes down to liking yourself. Do you think that you're basically a good person, and feel comfortable with yourself? If so, then your sense of self-worth is in pretty good shape.

But self-worth is about more than just how you see yourself. We're social beings, after all, and self-esteem is closely linked to the esteem in which others hold us. Our judgments about ourselves often factor in the judgements of others. If others like us and hold us in high regard, we have what researchers call relational social value.

People with relational social value tend to have close relationships with others, and they tend to be valued in those relationships. The higher our relational social value, the higher our sense of self-worth.

The other part of self-esteem is mastery. Mastery is the extent to which you can act intentionally, achieve your goals, and exercise your will. It comes down to feeling like a competent human being. But just like self-worth, our sense of mastery depends partly on how others judge us. That's where another kind of social value – instrumental social value – comes in. That's the degree to which others see us as having qualities that are important for the common good.

Of course, you'll have more mastery in some areas of your life than others. If you repeatedly encounter obstacles when trying to achieve your goals, you may begin to feel incompetent and insecure. On the other hand, if you're consistently able to achieve your goals, you'll feel increasingly confident, which tends to create an upward spiral. The result: an overall sense of mastery.

Exploration enables you to grow as a person.

Have you ever watched children at play? If you have, you've surely noticed how absorbed they become in their games, approaching the world with curiosity and fascination, as though life were one big adventure.

Sadly enough, our adventuresome nature tends to fade in adulthood. As we grow up, our playfulness and wonder begin to wane. This is a shame, because exploration has many benefits. For one, it's how we learn more about the world. It can also help us sweep away our fears and anxieties.

If we want to keep growing and developing, we should take a tip from children and treat life like a new land to be explored.

The key message here is: Exploration enables you to grow as a person.

So what exactly is exploration? Well, it's the desire to seek out unfamiliar information and experiences.

There are two types of exploration. One is known as behavioral exploration. The other is called cognitive exploration. Let's break each of these types down a bit, starting with behavioral exploration.

Behavioral exploration has two components: social exploration and adventure-seeking.

Let's talk about social exploration first. It's when we have a sincere interest in other people's lives and are curious about what they're thinking. It's also what drives us to make new friends, take part in discussions, or seek out new experiences. It's about engaging with people in a way that helps us learn more about them and the world.

So what about adventure-seeking? Well, people who seek adventure are often driven by the desire to learn and grow, to overcome challenges and learn new skills. Most people will look at a mountain and will feel nervous about climbing it. But adventure-seekers master their fear. They climb the mountain. And they're more resilient and tolerant of stress because of it.

But you don't need to scale mountains to be an explorer. And this is where cognitive exploration comes in. It's the kind of exploring you do with your senses and your mind.

Cognitive exploration itself has two parts. One is openness to experience. This involves things like appreciating beauty, getting absorbed in activities, and enjoying artistic pursuits. People who are open to experiences in this way also tend to be intuitive, empathetic, and in touch with their emotions.

The second part is intellectual. It comes down to reasoning and understanding the world through abstract thought. It's the desire to learn new information and discover new ideas. If you enjoy intellectual challenges and philosophical discussions, then you're an intellectual explorer.

Love is more fulfilling when it's not based on a deficiency.

In conversations with friends, in popular culture, even in psychology research, love tends to be defined in negative terms. We think of love as a lack. Love is something people want, something they long for, something that must be found out there. Finding love means receiving love.

But the people who feel that they've truly found love, the people who don't experience love primarily as a lack, are those who give love.

This just goes to show that we can move beyond the love-as-lack definition, and become capable of turning our love outward.

The key message here is: Love is more fulfilling when it's not based on a deficiency.

In his writings, Maslow distinguished between deficiency-love, or D-love for short, and love for a person's whole being. He called this latter type of love B-love. D-love is something we feel like we have to search and strive for. It's a need, and it has to be satisfied.

But that's not how B-love works. People who love in this way don't need to receive much love at all – their love is not about what's missing from their lives. Instead, they're focused on admiring others and giving.

It's a shift from regarding love as something to be gotten to seeing it as something to be given, from depending on others and being rewarded with their love to loving the world at large.

So how do people who practice B-love act?

For one, they tend to be driven by self-transcendent values. B-loving people are also notable for high levels of tolerance, benevolence, and trustworthiness. They have character traits like kindness, humility, and forgiveness. Other people love being around them. But B-loving people are also able to look after their own needs and assert themselves when necessary – they just do it in a way that remains caring and considerate of others.

Above all, B-loving people are able to integrate two aspects of human existence that might seem contradictory: agency and communion. Agency involves independence and separation from others. It's about how much you're able to achieve your own goals and assert yourself. In contrast, community is about contact, openness and participation – being together with others.

B-loving people manage to bring both aspects into harmony. They do this by going beyond the need to receive love, maintaining high levels of self-reliance while also staying engaged in satisfying relationships.

Purpose is what gives meaning to our lives.

You might have heard about Greta Thunberg, the young climate-change activist. She's become a bit of a superstar. But she's the first to admit that she wasn't always so active, and she definitely wasn't always a superstar. For most of her teenage years, she struggled to make friends and spent a lot of time sitting alone in her room feeling sorry for herself.

Hard to believe, considering the confident young woman she's become. So what led to her transformation?

She found a purpose in life.

The key message here is: Purpose is what gives meaning to our lives.

A purpose is a sort of focal point. It's the center of your life, around which you can organize all your actions so that each has significance. It also gives you energy to pursue your goals and encourages perseverance.

Purpose often means having a calling – an overwhelming urge to follow a particular path in life. And for many, that calling is closely linked to work. So ask yourself, How do I see my work? Is it just a way to make money? Or do you find it interesting, but only if you make progress and get that promotion? Or is it the most important part of your life, something that you would do even if you didn't need the money? The closer you are to seeing your work as a calling, as something you'd do regardless of pay, the more likely you are to be satisfied – not just with your job, but with your life in general.

But what if you don't have a calling? Or what if you have one, but you lack the resources to pursue it? If that's your situation, don't fret.

There are steps you can take to make the pursuit of your goals easier.

First, choose wisely. When you choose goals that focus on growth – like self-improvement, creativity, or making the world a better place – pursuing them will tend to bring a feeling of well-being, which often isn't the case when you strive merely for money, power, or popularity.

Second, choose for the right reasons. That means looking for goals that feel meaningful on a deep level. The most worthy goal won't give you a sense of purpose if it doesn't mean anything to you. The more your goals resonate with you, the more your motivation increases – and the more likely you'll be to achieve them.

Peak experiences enhance your sense of self and your connection with the world.

Imagine you're on a hike in Arizona. You're there to see one of the world's natural wonders: the Grand Canyon. It's summer, and it's hot, and you've been hiking for hours – and then, suddenly, you're there. The massive canyon – it's bigger than you ever could have imagined! – stretches out before you. For a moment, you forget your surroundings. You forget that you're you. As you gaze out at that strange and wonderful vastness, you feel as though you've become one with the landscape.

Experiences like these are what happy memories are made of. But, beyond that, they are also a crucial component of self-actualization.

The key message here is: Peak experiences enhance your sense of self and your connection with the world.

That feeling you had at the lip of the Grand Canyon – that feeling of oneness with nature and the whole of existence – is what the author calls a peak experience. These are experiences of heightened beauty, wonder, joy, or serenity. Research suggests that peak experiences are great for mental health. They increase motivation and a sense of purpose, make relationships more satisfying, reduce fear of death and encourage personal growth.

And all peak experiences have one thing in common: self-loss.

Now, there are two types of self-loss.

One takes place when we're in the grip of insecurity. We feel unsure of ourselves or of our identity. This kind of self-loss is frightening

33

and can make the world seem bizarre and unreal.

The other kind of self-loss – the kind induced by peak experiences – is another matter altogether. It brings a deepened sense of connection with the world – a feeling of openness and curiosity. It's a paradox: the more the self dissolves and seems to merge with the world, the more self-actualized one feels.

There's one word that's often used in connection with peak experiences: awe. A feeling of awe can be inspired by vastness, like a view of the ocean or of the Grand Canyon. But it can also be conceptual. For example, contemplating eternity may inspire awe. The puzzling thing about awe is that it combines feelings that don't usually go together, such as fear and ecstasy.

Yes, although awe involves fear, people who experience it usually describe their experience as strongly positive.

And being filled with awe is good for you. Studies show that people who experience awe have increased life satisfaction; they also tend to be more generous and less aggressive.

Transcendence involves your entire being.

Now that you know about peak experiences, you might think that you can't go any higher. But it's actually possible to reach beyond the peak — and that's where transcendence comes in.

Transcendence is an elusive idea, and means many different things to many different people. In a 1969 paper about its meaning, Maslow came up with 35 ways to define the term. It included a great variety of concepts, from loss of self-consciousness to acceptance of the natural world to experiencing cosmic consciousness.

Which is the real transcendence?

Well, that's not quite the right question to ask. Transcendence is not just one aspect of your life – it's about the entirety of your existence.

The key message here is: Transcendence involves your entire being.

Transcendence is not a goal that you can simply achieve once and for all; rather, it's an ideal that can guide you. It's about being the best version of yourself, mobilizing all your resources in service of this version, and integrating them in a way that raises the standard for the whole of humanity.

Who are the people who do this?

Anyone can have a peak experience, regardless of what motivates that person in life. But people who are transcenders are not just striving for happiness, health, or personal growth. Instead, they're driven by transcendent values and have a vision for the whole of humanity.

Transcendent values leave deficiency needs behind. They're what you can aspire to when you're no longer motivated by lack, whether a lack of self-esteem or a lack of love. And they also exceed self-fulfillment. Instead, people motivated by transcendent values are devoted to a calling beyond themselves. This can include ideals like justice, truth, meaning, goodness, or beauty.

The paradox is that transcenders are not necessarily happy. They may often feel frustrated when they can't realize their vision, or feel sadness about things like human cruelty. But they're also better able to integrate the good and the bad sides of life, and to feel less regret.

In short, they integrate all aspects of human existence. They have the ability to look at the multiplicity of human needs in a nonjudgmental way, and see them not as conflicting, but as part of a harmonious whole.

Experiencing transcendence means accepting different perspectives, and being open to challenges and aware of the uncertainty inherent in human life.

SUMMARY KEYPOINT:

The key message in these blinks:

Human needs are all closely connected, and the greatest sense of well-being and fulfilment comes when we can integrate them into a healthy whole. With our needs integrated, we have a base for growth and self-actualization. We open ourselves to transcendent experiences and the possibility of becoming the best selves we can be.

BLINKREAD

BlinkRead is dedicated to creating high-quality summaries of non-fiction books to help you through the bestseller list each week!

We cover books in self-help, business, personal development, science & technology, health & fitness, history, and memoir/biography. Our books are expertly written and professionally edited to provide top-notch content. We're here to help you decide which books to invest your time and money reading.

Absorb everything you need to know in 20 minutes or less!

We release new summaries each and every week, so join our mailing list to stay up-to-date and get free summaries right in your inbox!

CPSIA information can be obtained
at www.ICGtesting.com
Printed in the USA
BVHW090911220822
645173BV00010B/300

9 798667 601425